ISBN 978-1-333-92457-7
PIBN 10645754

1 MONTH OF FREE READING

at

www.ForgottenBooks.com

By purchasing this book you are eligible for one month membership to ForgottenBooks.com, giving you unlimited access to our entire collection of over 1,000,000 titles via our web site and mobile apps.

To claim your free month visit:

www.forgottenbooks.com/free645754

English
Français
Deutsche
Italiano
Español
Português

www.forgottenbooks.com

Mythology Photography **Fiction**
Fishing Christianity **Art** Cooking
Essays Buddhism Freemasonry
Medicine **Biology** Music **Ancient**
Egypt Evolution Carpentry Physics
Dance Geology **Mathematics** Fitness
Shakespeare **Folklore** Yoga Marketing
Confidence Immortality Biographies
Poetry **Psychology** Witchcraft
Electronics Chemistry History **Law**
Accounting **Philosophy** Anthropology
Alchemy Drama Quantum Mechanics
Atheism Sexual Health **Ancient History**
Entrepreneurship Languages Sport
Paleontology Needlework Islam
Metaphysics Investment Archaeology
Parenting Statistics Criminology
Motivational

THE
WESTERN FRONT

Drawings by
MUIRHEAD BONE

VOLUME TWO

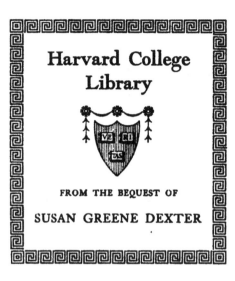

THE
WESTERN FRONT

DRAWINGS BY
MUIRHEAD BONE

THE SOMME BATTLEFIELD.

THE main Anglo-German battlefield of 1916 is a little range of chalk down or blunt hill. It is ten miles long and seven miles wide, and its watershed runs from north-west to south-east—from near Thiepval, above the small river Ancre, to Combles, four miles to the north of the canalised Somme. This summit ridge is not quite 500 feet high—about as high as the Hog's Back in Surrey. The south-western slope of the range is rather steeper and more broken up into terraces and lateral ridges and defiles than the north-eastern slope. There is no real escarpment, but enough difference to make the south-western slope the harder to attack.

Small as this ridge is, it is the highest ground, in these parts, between the Belgian plain and the main plain of Northern France. It is crossed at right angles by one great road, the famous French Route Nationale that runs nearly dead straight from Rouen, through Amiens, to Valenciennes, and so leads on to Brussels by Mons. On the battlefield, between Albert and Bapaume, it reaches the highest point above the sea in all its long course, at a spot where a heap of powdered brick and masonry, forty yards off to the north, marks the site of the Windmill of

Pozières, one of those solitary buildings to which, like Falfemont Farm and the Abbey at Eaucourt, the war has brought death and immortality.

From this road, at one point or another, you can see most of the places that were made famous in 1916. A mile and a half from Albert, as you go out north-eastward, you spy in a hollow below you a whitish sprinkling of mixed mud, brick-dust and lime, the remains of La Boisselle, on the right of the road. On its left a second grey patch is the site of Ovillers. Beyond La Boisselle Contalmaison is just out of sight behind a shoulder of hill. Nearly all the most hard-fought woods are in sight—High Wood on the sky-line, and Delville Wood larger on its right, and then in succession, with sharp intervals of bareness between them, the woods of Bazentin, Mametz and Fricourt. Above them and more distant are the dense trees that have Maricourt and the French troops at their feet, and, high on their right, the thin file of trees shading the road that runs from Albert, past Carnoy and Cléry, to Peronne. You walk on for three miles and may not observe that you have passed through Pozières, so similar are raw chalk and builder's lime, raw clay and powdered brick, when weeds grow thick over both. But the great road—strangely declined into a rough field track—begins to fall away before you, and new prospects to open—Courcelette and Martinpuich almost at your feet, and straight beyond them the church and town hall of Bapaume at the end of the long avenue of roadside trees. Looking left you see, two miles away, the western end of the summit ridge, the last point upon it from which the Germans were driven; so that, even after the fall of Thiepval, a shell would sometimes come from the Schwaben Redoubt to remind unwary walkers at Pozières Windmill that enemy eyes still watched the lost ground.

Among the wreckage of the countryside you can detect the traces of old standing comfort and rustic wealth. The many wayside windmills show you how much corn was grown. In size and plan they are curiously like the mighty stone dovecotes of Fifeshire. Almost as frequent as ruined windmills are ruined sugar refineries, standing a little detached in the fields, like the one at Courcelette, for which armies fought as they fought for the neighbouring windmill. Beet was the next crop to grain. There were little industries, too, like the making of buttons for shirts at Fricourt, where you see by the road small refuse heaps of old oyster shells with many round holes where the little discs have been cut cleanly out of the mother-of-pearl, though all other trace of the factories has vanished. Each village commune had its wood, with certain rights for the members of the commune to take timber; Fricourt Wood at the doors of Fricourt, Mametz Wood rather far from Mametz, as there was no good wood nearer. All these woods were well fenced and kept up, like patches of hedged cover dotted over a park. It was a good country to live in, and good men came from it. The French Army Corps that drew on these villages for recruits has won honour beyond all other French Corps in the battle of the Somme.

Many skilled writers have tried to describe the aghast look of these fields where the battle had passed over them. But every new visitor says the same thing—that they had not succeeded; no eloquence has yet conveyed the disquieting strangeness of the portent. You can enumerate many ugly and queer freaks of the destroying powers—the villages not only planed off the face of the earth but rooted out of it, house by house, like bits of old teeth; the thin brakes of black stumps that used to be woods, the old graveyards wrecked like kicked ant-heaps, the tilth so disembowelled by shells that most of the good upper mould created by centuries of the work of worms and men is buried out of sight and the unwrought primeval subsoil lies on the top; the sowing of the whole ground with a new kind of dragon's teeth—unexploded shells that the plough may yet detonate, and bombs that may let themselves off if their safety pins rust away sooner than the springs within. But no piling up of sinister detail can express the sombre and malign quality of the battlefield landscape as a whole. "It makes a goblin of the sun"—or it might if it were not peopled in every part with beings so reassuringly and engagingly human, sane and reconstructive as British soldiers.

G. H. Q., France.
January, 1917.

AMIENS CATHEDRAL

The "Parthenon of Gothic Architecture" is seen in this exquisitely delicate and sensitive drawing from the south-east, with the lovely rose window of the south transept partly in view on the left. The wooden spire, which Ruskin called " the pretty caprice of a village carpenter," looks finer in the drawing than in the original, the relative flimsiness of the material being less apparent. Nothing is lost by the intervention of the foreground houses, as the façade of the south transept, like the famous west front and the choir stalls, is sheathed with sandbags to a height of thirty or forty feet for protection against German bombs. Patrolling French aeroplanes are seen in the sky.

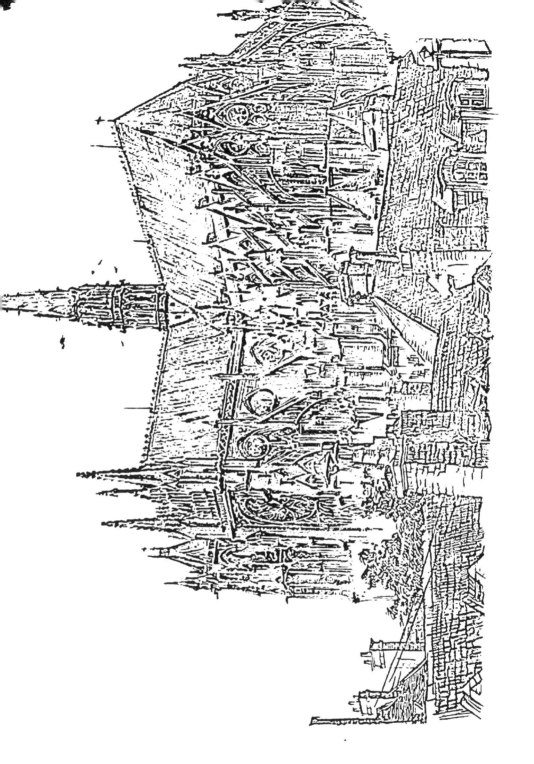

THE VIRGIN OF MONTAUBAN

An image which strangely escaped destruction during the time when the village of Montauban, now utterly erased, was being shelled successively by British and German guns. By a similar caprice of fate the Virgin of Carençy, now enshrined in a little chapel in the French military cemetery at Villers-aux-Bois, received only some shot wounds when the village was destroyed during the French advance towards Lens in 1915.

A SKETCH IN ALBERT

Albert, as a whole, is wrecked to the degree shown in this drawing. The ·building in the middle distance, on the right of the road, with its roof timbers exposed, is a wrecked factory, and many hundreds of bicycles and sewing machines now make an extraordinary tangle of twisted and broken metal in its basement.

TAKING THE WOUNDED ON BOARD

Wounded men from the Somme, ordered to England by the Medical Officer commanding the General or Stationary Hospital in which each man has been a patient, are being put on board a hospital ship at the base. In the centre of the foreground is seen the timber framework of the ship's large red cross of electric lights. With this, and a tier of some sixty green lights running from stem to stern, a hospital ship at night is a beautiful as well as unmistakeable object at sea.

"WALKING WOUNDED" SLEEPING ON DECK

The best place to sleep, on a summer night in a full hospital ship, for a man whose wound is not grave enough to cause serious "shock" and consequent need of much artificial warming.

"WALKING WOUNDED" ON A HOSPITAL SHIP

This drawing was done in the warm early autumn of 1916. All "walking wounded" wear lifebelts, if their injuries permit, during the Channel crossing, and each "stretcher case" has a lifebelt under his pillow, if not on. The necessity for this, in a war with Germany, has been proved by the fate of too many of our hospital ships.

"WALKING WOUNDED" ON A HOSPITAL SHIP

The deck of a British hospital ship is one of the most cheerful places in the world. Every man is at rest after toil, is about to see friends after separation, can smoke when he likes, and has in every other man on board a companion with whom endless reminiscences can be exchanged, and perhaps the merits and demerits of the Ypres salient, or the most advantageous use of "tanks," warmly debated, as is the custom of privates of the New Army. Silent or vocal, a great beatitude fills the vessel.

A MAIN APPROACH TO THE BRITISH FRONT

The canvas screen on the left marks a place where the road had been under enemy observation. A "sausage," or stationary observation balloon, is seen above the road. "Sausages" are not pretty. They exhibit, at various stages of inflation, the various shapes taken by a maggot partly uncurled. But the work done from them, besides being always disagreeable and often risky, is extremely valuable.

"ROAD LIABLE TO BE SHELLED"

A stretch of high-road which was under enemy observation when drawn. Such roads are, of course, only used with due caution. The whole drawing is remarkably instinct with the artist's sense of a malign invisible presence—a "terror that walketh by noonday"—infesting the sunny vacant length of the forbidden road.

Bone

ROAD CLOSED
TO ALL TRAFFIC
DURING DAYLIGHT

Bone

TROUBLE ON THE ROAD

War has its tyre troubles, as peace has. In this case the lack of a spare wheel, and the consequent necessity for changing an inner tube, had the compensation of giving the artist time to make the drawing.

BRITISH TROOPS ON THE MARCH TO THE SOMME

A typical Picardy landscape behind the frontal zone of destruction. The crescent-shaped line of troops and transport on the road is a small fraction of a Division moving up to take its place in the front line.

A SKETCH AT CONTALMAISON

The place is Contalmaison, but the drawing has caught the spirit of the whole of the shattered country-side recaptured this year.

ON THE SOMME : SAUSAGE BALLOONS

A typical winter scene on the Somme battlefield. The nearer " sausage," or captive observation balloon, is being run out to its proper height for work, by unwinding its cable from a reel on the ground. The further balloon is already moored high enough and its observer, alone in the small hanging cage, is at work with his map, telescope and telephone.

A WRECKED AEROPLANE NEAR ALBERT

A casualty in the R.F.C. The smashed biplane and the retreating stretcher party on the right explain themselves. On the left, Albert church, to the right of a tall factory chimney, is seen in the distance.

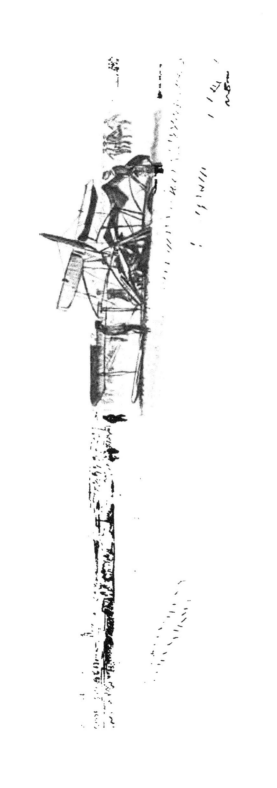

A MESS OF THE ROYAL FLYING CORPS

The Officers' mess at the most advanced station of the Royal Flying Corps on the Somme front. The great tent was designed as an aeroplane hangar. An R.F.C. mess usually has an atmosphere of its own. There is more variety of apparel than at other messes; there are more dogs; personal mascots abound, and in many ways there is more expression of individual choice or peculiarity than elsewhere—corresponding, perhaps, to the more individual character of a flying officer's work and responsibilities and to the temperament which leads to success in flying. The officers are drawn from all sorts of regiments, and each continues to wear his regimental badge. It is winter, and the second figure from the left is wearing a fur jacket.

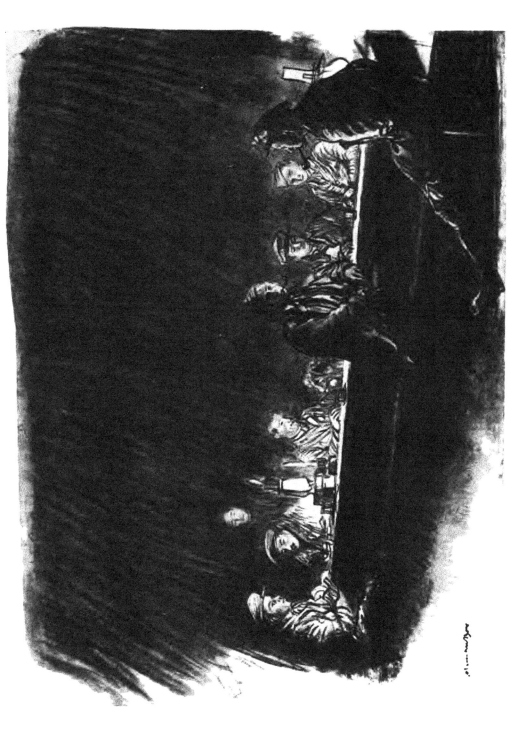

WATCHING OUR ARTILLERY FIRE ON TRONES WOOD FROM MONTAUBAN

The drawing expresses well the singular aspect of the parts of the battlefield where artillery fire was heavy and where the conical holes made in the ground by high explosive shells were consequently close together. At a later stage these separate pock-marks overlap, like the pits in confluent small-pox, and the whole of the shelled ground becomes soft and loose, as though raked deeply but unevenly. In the distance the detached higher puffs of smoke from bursting shrapnel are distinguishable from the rising clouds of smoke from high-explosive shells.

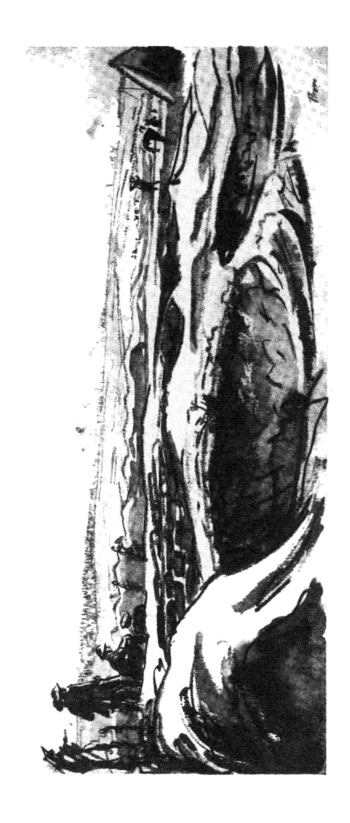

IN THE REGAINED TERRITORY

Both the places drawn were in German hands until July. The first drawing is of a cemetery found behind the old German front line near Fricourt. There were many imperfectly marked German graves near these. They have since been marked, as many thousands of hurriedly made British graves have been, with wooden crosses and metal inscriptions by our Graves' Registration and Inquiries Units.

The second drawing, with a helmeted sentry at the sand-bagged entrance to a dug-out, conveys the sinister air of a village destroyed, but not quite effaced, by shell-fire.

A V.A.D. REST STATION

At a base railway station in France. Between the arrivals of hospital trains from the front the V.A.D. workers occupy themselves in the "dispensary" in rolling bandages or preparing hot cocoa and other food for the wounded or sick men who will pass through the station.

The Dispensary, V.A.D. Rest Station

A GATEWAY AT ARRAS

A few hundred yards from this gate the Anglo-French treaty of peace was signed after Agincourt. Part of the city's later history is written in the curious and beautiful Spanish architecture of its chief squares. It is now in the middle stage of destruction: almost every building is shattered or injured, but enough is standing to make the empty city seem still sensitive, in its very stones, under the enemy's random shellfire.

OUTSIDE ARRAS, NEAR THE GERMAN LINES

At Arras the Germans always seem very near you. In fact they are. No other famous town in the Allies' hands has a German front trench in its suburbs ; nowhere do the two front trenches come so close to each other. The result is a subtle quality of apprehensiveness in the atmosphere of the silent empty city. It seems like someone standing on tiptoe, peering and listening, in a solitary place, for some vague unseen danger, or like a horse nervously pricking its ears, you cannot tell why. This tingle of uncanny dread has been conveyed with remarkable success in this figureless but haunted landscape.

WATCHING GERMAN PRISONERS

British soldiers watching recently captured Germans on their way down from the front to an Army Corps "cage." Until removed to the base our prisoners are well housed in huts or tents in a kind of compound fenced with barbed wire and placed well outside the range of their friends' artillery. There are no attempts at escape. Our men, behind the front line, always watch the arrival of new prisoners with silent curiosity. Those of our soldiers who have themselves fought with the Germans, and captured them, usually befriend them with cigarettes and drinks from water-bottles.

ON THE SOMME: "MUD"

At a camp, near Albert, whose Church, with the image knocked awry, is seen to the right. With the permission of the officer on the left some soldiers are fishing in the mud for such fragments of old timber, boxes and tins as may be of use to them in their field housekeeping, though they are not worth collecting for deposit at the official Salvage Dumps.

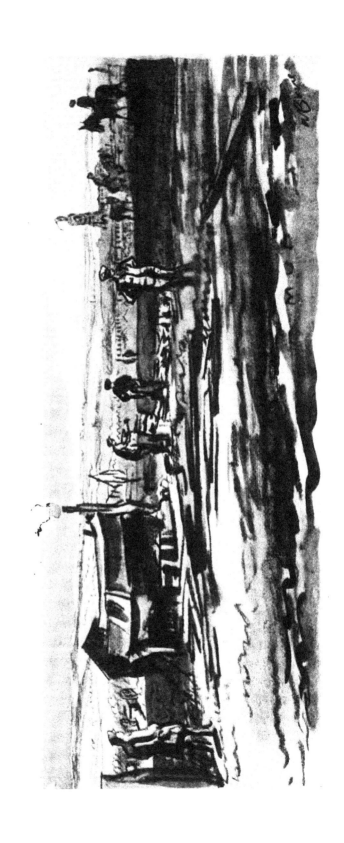

DESERTS

N France the war has made several kinds of desert, each with a quality of its own, derived from the way in which it was made. Verdun I have not seen. Of the other deserts the first in date was that of the Somme battlefield. In earlier parts of the "Western ⟨Fron⟩t" it has been drawn, in sample, several times. It spreads so far in bulk, it can only be seen from the air. It is the most evenly ⟨spread⟩ed of all these made deserts. From the Ancre to the Santerre you ⟨pass⟩ through different kinds of landscape. There are little hills, river ⟨mea⟩dows, and a high grain-bearing flat. Over them all there was laid in ⟨191⟩ a kind of spotted brown counterpane or mask which makes them ⟨lo⟩ok alike. The spots on this cloth are dense along its middle and ⟨grow⟩ less dense towards its fringe all round. To an eye that knew the ⟨coun⟩try well before the war, it must seem now as if the villages, with all ⟨the⟩ differences of look, and the various greens or yellows of the old ⟨field⟩s, must surely be hidden under this spotted coverlet. But really ⟨they⟩ are not there, and the brown is that of bare and raw earth, and the ⟨spot⟩s are shell-holes.

The next kind of desert was made by the enemy, partly at leisure and partly in haste, when he fell back between the battles of the Somme and of Arras. Here there is nothing that seems to express the indiscriminate fury traditionally ascribed to war. The Somme battle-field really does look as if some irresistible angel of death and demolition had breathed in the face of the whole country and its occupants. Nothing has been let off, neither village nor field, nor wood, nor even the graves of the dead. It might have looked like this on the site of the cities of the plain, after the catastrophe. In the country from which the Germans did not wait to be driven the havoc is less exhaustive, more selective, more obviously purposeful in detail; each unit of destructive force employed has gone, on the average, much further, a little gun-cotton or dynamite doing the important part of the work of a thousand shells. In the fields there are few shell-holes; many fields, when we took them, were ploughed and harrowed and ready for sowing. The roadside trees are not roughly broken across and shredded by shells aimed at something else, but are cut clean through with the saw, two feet from the ground. The houses are not battered in from without by many fortuitous hits, but are methodically blown outwards from within by sufficient charges of some high explosive placed against the inside of the walls. In a house wrecked by shell-fire the roof is usually one of the first parts to go ; in a house demolished in the German manner the walls are knocked out from under the roof and lie on the ground outside, as heaps of brick and lime, and the roof settles down, often almost intact and erect, on the ground inside these ruins, with a grotesque likeness to a hat placed on the ground.

At first sight all this wrecking looks cold-blooded. The German Staff defends it as being cold-blooded. It was, the Staff say, the cold-blooded execution of the legitimate tactical manœuvre of giving to a pursuing enemy a desert to live in and to attack from. But, when you look into the German demolitions between the Scarpe and the Aisne, you feel that many things here were done not in cold blood but in something worse. When you find houses, of some use as billets, left standing, but all the heads chipped off the little figures of angels and saints in the reredos of an ancient church, you cannot quite feel that military necessity accounts for it all.

As you go eastward across the wilderness, six miles south of Arras, you pass at first along roads beside which every tree and telegraph post have been carefully felled, through villages in which no house or tree has been spared which could shelter a man from the weather at night or from aeroplane observation by day. At each cross-road a mine has been blown so as to hamper pursuit. Along the first part of your way it is all done deliberately and completely. But when you have passed through the ruins of Boisieux-au-Mont and Boisieux-St.-Marc you begin to see signs of hurry. Some of the trees here have escaped felling. Many houses here have only been maimed, not destroyed. Cross-roads occur at which you do not have to traverse the bed of a crater or coast round its lip. You see that here the pursuit had grown hot; there was not time to do all that military expediency required. But for one thing, not so required, time did not fail; it was always found. Cottage gardens, with their little orchards of espalier and small standard fruit trees, their toy-like summer-houses and old box edging and slowly grown wistaria, were always laid waste with a careful, circumstantial malignity which seems still to grin out at you venomously from the wreckage of these inoffensive little pleasaunces.

The craving to give gratuitous pain to unknown individual enemies is a form of baseness not often found among soldiers fighting in the front line, in this or any other war between white men. It is a disease, in the main, of non-combatants. But German commanders cannot be acquitted of having given way to this impulse of unknightly ill-nature, in the chagrin of last winter's retreat. Where they had not the time both to impede the pursuing British army and also to cut down the village priest's half-grown cherry trees, or to prevent some old French cottager from ever sitting in her little yew-tree arbour again, then these practitioners of scientific war really seem to have thrown Clausewitz to the winds and concentrated their forces against priest and old woman. Hot blood and foul blood, not cold.

A third kind of desert was made on part of the new battlefield of Arras. It resembles the first described here in so far as it was mainly made by shell-fire, bombs and mines. But it has a touch of resemblance to the second in the rather more obvious purposefulness of each stroke of destruction. There is more emphasis and selection. On the cloth thrown over the Arras battlefield the pattern of spots is not so even as that on the Somme. Even at its centre the spots are dense at one point and sparse at another. And you can nearly always see why they are specially dense. They cluster and crowd one another round the strong points and lines of old German defences, while spaces less formidably held, or not held at all, by the enemy were left almost unmarked by us during the first days of rapid advance. The difference is mainly due to the quite simple reason that our artillery fire is more precise in 1917 than it was in 1916. It makes better—that is, smaller—groups of shell-holes round the marks at which it aims.

G. H. Q., France.

June, 1917.

CHÂTEAU NEAR BRIE

An ancient fortified and moated house at Happlincourt. It had been to some extent injured by Allied shell-fire when the Germans quitted it on their retreat. They blew up parts of it with explosive charges. The waters of the moat are drawn from the Somme, which flows past the house on its east.

XXII

THE GREAT CRATER, ATHIES

The largest of several craters made by the Germans in the roads at or near Athies before their flight. The ruined house belonged to the owner of a sugar refinery in the place. The house was without architectural interest, but had a finely planted garden.

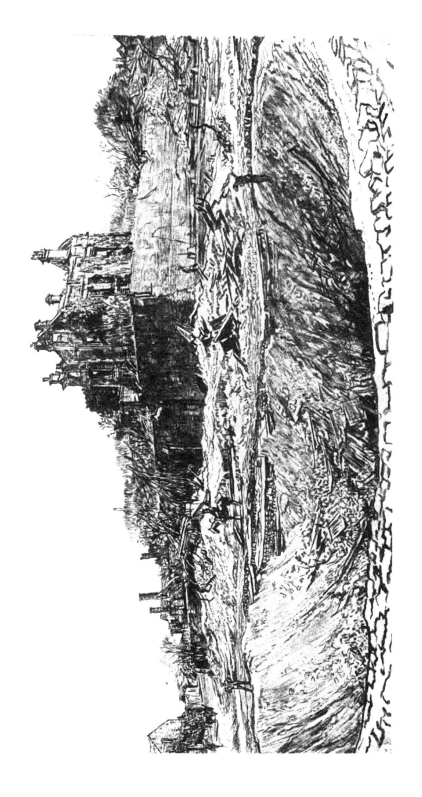

XXIII

THE CHURCH OF ATHIES

A typical scene in the area laid waste by the retreating Germans. All the wreckage seen here was done by hand or with demolition charges of high explosive. The land in the foreground was the parish priest's garden. All the trees were fruit trees and they have all been sawn through or felled with the axe. The sap was rising strongly in them at the time and they have put forth many blossoms, for the last time, as they lie rootless on the ground. The church was blown up from within, but some caprice in the action of the explosives has spared a beautiful fourteenth century porch.

XXIV

DÉNIECOURT CHÂTEAU, ESTRÉES

The site of the Château is marked by the large heap of ruins near the centre of the drawing. It was used for head-quarters by Germans, French and British in succession. In the space on the left of the Château are some German soldiers' graves. Fastened to a tree on the right is the notice "Do not loiter here," which is often seen in places exposed to shell fire.

THE ORANGERY, DÉNIÉCOURT CHÂTEAU

In Northern France, as in England, an orangery was one of the pleasant things included in the plan of many of the older country houses. Of the orangery at Déniécourt— one of the villages recovered by the French from the Germans last year—nothing remains but a few broken pots and fragments of wood and ironwork.

XXVI

ECCE SIGNUM

A shell has struck a large crucifix standing in a rural cemetery which, like many others, contains a small proportion of older civilian graves and a large proportion of new graves of soldiers.

A SUGAR FACTORY IN THE SANTERRE

Sugar beet is the chief farm product of the part of France which includes the Somme and Arras battlefields, the damp Channel climate being better for roots than for fruit or grain, while the nearness of the Pas de Calais coal field cheapens the extraction of sugar and alcohol from the beet. The waste products of these processes feed a number of cattle out of proportion to the pasture land of the district, and the presence of so many cattle secures the manuring of the beet fields. Thanks to this system of interdependencies, sugar refineries abounded on all the northern battlefields of the Western front. Great piles of broken and twisted machinery, lying between ruined walls, show the energy with which many of these factories, which usually stand a little apart from villages, have been attacked and defended.

AN OLD "O. P."

In a tree on the left is seen the remaining woodwork of an old "O. P.," "O Pip," or Observation Post for artillery, with the means of access to it. In the centre, receding from the spectator, is a line of narrow gauge railway running up to the trenches. The Allied advance of this year has rendered this "O. P." obsolete, so that it can safely be shown in a published drawing.

VILLERS CARBONNEL

Villers Carbonnel was a village near the western verge of the territory evacuated by the Germans early in 1917. It had suffered some injury from shell-fire in 1916, and was utterly wrecked by the Germans before they left it.

A ROSE GARDEN

A rare specimen of the not quite complete destruction by the Germans of every amenity in the country which they had to leave in the winter of 1916-17. The arches on which the roses had been trained are still standing, though knocked about, and the lines of the box edging can be traced, though the beauty of the old formal garden is spoilt past restoration. The Germans wrecked the church behind the garden by means of charges of explosives placed inside its walls.

XXX

A GERMAN H.Q.

The remains of the Château of Damery, a fine old house
a little way behind the German front line after the battle
of the Somme.   The enemy used its basement as a head-
quarters; the entrance may be seen at the ground level.
The damage seen was caused by shell-fire.   The German
devastations began a little further behind their front.

THE CHÂTEAU, FOUCAUCOURT

This country house stood about a mile and a half behind the Allied front line before the battle of the Somme. It was shattered by German shells. The trees, also mutilated by shell-fire, have made valiant efforts to revive in the spring of 1917. Affixed to a tree on the left there remains a billeting officer's notice of the amount of accommodation available for troops in the cellars of the house.

XXXII

A RUINED TRENCH : MONT ST. ELOI
IN THE DISTANCE

Mont St. Eloi was one of the finest view-points along the old front. There was an ancient abbey on the top of the hill, and the two irregular stems of masonry seen in the drawing are the remains of two tall towers added to it in the eighteenth century. Below the hill, and on the left of the ruin, the French carried the little village of La Targette, in 1915, in one of the most gallant and bloodiest assaults of the war. The German front line has now ebbed far away from the hill, but the position of the front is nearly always indicated roughly by an irregular line of shell bursts.

XXXIII

HERBÉCOURT CHURCH

In the country recovered by the French from the Germans, south of the Somme, in 1916. The damage done here, as at the neighbouring Assevillers, was by shell-fire. A comparison of this drawing with that of " The Church of Assevillers " shows how capriciously destruction goes about its work. At Herbécourt a single pillar remains, as a kind of fortuitous monument of the rest of the church.

XXXIV

THE CHURCH OF ASSEVILLERS

Assevillers is a village south-west of Péronne. The French won it back from the Germans in the summer of 1916, and it was close to the line taken over by British troops from the French in the following winter. The church had then been destroyed by shell-fire. Near Assevillers there was to be seen for some months at the beginning of 1917 the most remarkable of many ravaged village cemeteries; monuments, coffins and bones were all displaced, broken and mixed together by the explosions of shells among the graves.

XXXV

"OUT OF THE LINE"

When a Scottish Division comes out of the trenches to rest, one of its special joys is that of listening at ease to the regimental pipers. A group of typical warrant officers and senior non-commissioned officers of the Black Watch are here seen in full fruition of this delight. To appreciate rightly the music of the pipes an Englishman should hear it played to a Scots Battalion marching up to the front or to the thinned platoons marching westwards when relieved after a hard fight.

XXXVI

NEAR DOMPIERRE

The building which is here seen ruined by shell-fire had apparently been the farm-house of some well-to-do man with agriculture for his hobby. The broken gates were good ironwork, with the initials of the owner worked into their design, and the whole place must have worn a look of comfort and some handsomeness.

" INCONNU "

The grave of some officer or man whose body could not be identified is a common sight in this war, in which an unusually large percentage of casualties are caused by shell-fire and bombs, and some of the dead remain for a long time out of reach in No Man's Land. Some of the unknown are buried by their comrades, and some by their enemies, the graves bearing such inscriptions, in English, French, or German, as "Two unknown Germans buried here," "Unknown. He died for his country," or "Here rests an English soldier." The grave seen here was at the edge of a little wood near Estrées.

XXXVIII

MAIN STREET OF FLERS: SUNSET

The scene of a famous episode on September 15th, 1916, the day on which tanks first went into action. One tank, impulsively driven, made its way, ahead of our general advance, into the main street of Flers, followed by a cheering crowd of British infantry, and moved up and down the village, firing its machine guns, until the resistance of the enemy garrison ceased.

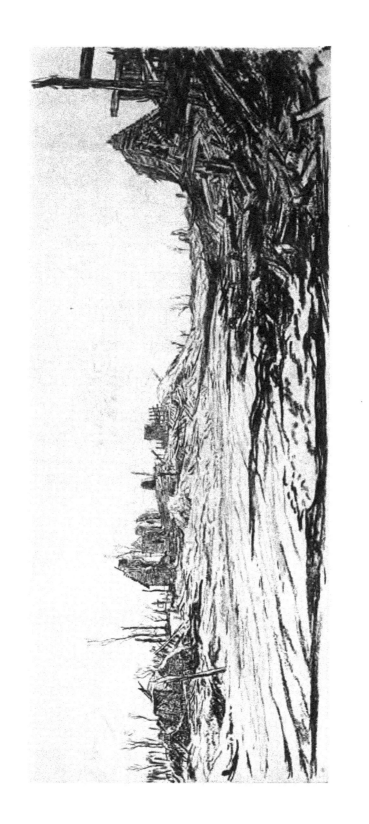

XXXIX

ROUEN

Like Innsbruck and Winchester, Rouen has the charm of
an ancient capital with the surroundings of a country town.
Here Joan of Arc was burnt and King John murdered
Prince Arthur; the walls defied our Henry V in Agincourt
year. Sea-going vessels steam 70 miles up the Seine—
and it is one of the most beautiful river journeys in Europe
—to the quay shown in the foreground of the drawing.
Rouen has more precious heirlooms of mediæval architecture than any other French city; it is "earthlier happy"
in the possession of a good damp climate for spinning
cotton, excellent shops, and a pleasant race-course, covered
at present by the tents and huts of a British military
hospital, administered from the grand stand.

XL

ON A HOSPITAL SHIP AT NIGHT : THE ORDERLY

The drawing was made on one of the smaller and less perfectly equipped hospital ships which have occasionally had to be called into the service during times of hard fighting. Like most night-sisters in hospitals, an R.A.M.C. orderly on night duty usually ties himself, as it were, with an elastic string, to a piece of literature, so that he can at once be drawn away from it by the needs of any of his patients, but springs back to his reading as soon as this pull is relaxed.

BEHIND THE FRONT

IMAGINE a company of our infantry coming out of the trenches to rest. From the zigzag crack in the earth, along which they have walked for two miles, they come to the surface close to a village. The village has holes in its eastern walls, but is not destroyed. Just as the company enter the main village street some German guns, groping about for some British guns which are not there, begin to search the village with shells. Other shells are falling pretty thickly on the road beyond the village. Along this road the troops will have to pass to their billets, in cellars under the ruins of houses a mile or two on. The village street runs north and south, parallel to the front. So the company commander orders his men to fall out and rest, under the lee of the houses on the east side of the street, and let the squall pass.

Everybody who comes from a trench is tired. The men, glad of any excuse for a halt, sit down on the cottage doorsteps and look at civilian life, which seems amusing and curious after a long tour of duty in trenches. Cottagers living on this the safe side of the street come to their doors and talk to the troops unconcernedly. One woman, seeing a boy of nineteen, with the looks of fifteen, badly tired, brings him some hot coffee. He wants to pay, but she laughs and says " Après la guerre. Après la guerre." Children are coming from school, each with its gas-mask slung at its side in a little satchel. Others are playing absorbedly in the middle of the street, German shells having long lost the interest of novelty, while the thrill of games is eternal. Nearly all the children are well fed and clothed, as a French child is till its parents starve. One child, very ragged, shuffles along past the men on the doorsteps, begging : " Souvenir jam, souvenir boulie " (bully beef). Two bolder spirits, about ten years old, requisition " Souvenir cigarette " with jovial assurance. Rebuked by a corporal who can speak French, one of the imps surveys this moralist's face with a finely assumed expression of horror, and says " Qu'il est laid ! " to the other. " Mon dieu, oui ! " the other replies. The corporal laughs and pays the desired tribute to the unconquerable wit of the Gaul.

The shells are coming in faster ; one or two of them bump against the backs of the houses in front of which the human comedy is going its way. Little pieces of shrapnel fall and rattle on the roofs. Some of the pieces slide down the slates and pitch over into the street. Women come out to doors and order children to " come in out of that," as British mothers do when it rains. On the western side of the street shutters are being put up, to keep the small stuff away from the glass ; householders, grumbling, descend into their cellars ; the last to go is a woman with whom an English sergeant has bargained for thirty cups of the very small beer of French Flanders, for his platoon. The contract completed, she lingers to show him, with the just pride of a collector, a large conical dent in her paved backyard—" The fifth of June last year, Sergeant—the largest shell that ever fell in this village." The enemy's fire is slackening now ; shutters begin to reopen ; the men swallow their beer, fall in, and jog on ; already the children are playing again in the street.

Most of the heads of households in places like this are widows with children, or wives of Frenchmen now in the field. They fear leaving home, or they do not know where else to go, and they can live by selling a small range of wares to the English soldiers ; bread, which the men like as a change from ration bread, though this is good ; chocolate, oranges, apples, sardines, candles, of which you cannot have too many in dug-outs and cellars ; picture post-cards, the most penetrative of all the merchandise of the front. Other women wash for our men, or keep small unofficial taverns with " English beer and stout " on a card in the window, and tables arranged round the wall of a room, where the men sit in warm semi-darkness at night and order their drinks in an Allied dialect, half French, half English. "Anchor a stoo, Miss; anchor a stoo," someone will say who wants a glass more of stout.

To-morrow, perhaps, the company that has passed will be marching off, much further westward, for its Divisional rest. As they pass remote villages, women and children will issue from cottages, carrying little trays of cakes and oranges slung from their necks, for sale to the men. They will trail along beside the marching column, sometimes for miles, awaiting the growth and renewal of appetite for their stock, with the patient eagerness of sea-gulls that follow an outgoing ship. In the evening the column may pass through a mining village near Béthune or Bruay and see streaming away from the pithead a crowd of elderly French miners, with whom our ex-miners in khaki, from Durham and Yorkshire, contrive to exchange good technical chaff.

In France, as in England, the war has caused a great industrial experiment to be made. An enormous number of people who used to do some particular kind of work before the war are now doing something else. Men who used to keep accounts or make chairs have charge of horses. Women who used to make lace at Arras, or table-cloths at Cambrai, now cut hair at Amiens or Rouen, or find new work of the factory kind in our army's big repair depots, where thousands of gas-masks and boots are mended each day, and French girls test, with swift precision, the straightness of British bayonets, on which much depends. They earn high wages and sing all the time. Wool weavers from Lille and linen weavers from Armentières, middle-aged men, work at the hutting of troops at a British base, directed by London contractors' foremen: "Tudsweet (tout de suite), with them planks, sonnies, compry?" a foreman will say when he wants a job done. Of course there is plenty, too, of that less sweeping redistribution of work which has always come with a war, since Porsena marched on Rome. In Artois and Picardy old men reap the harvests, and women drive ploughs, and boys wash sheep in the Canche as they did in the Umbro.

G.H.Q., France.
July, 1917.

XLI

PANORAMA FROM THE SCHERPENBERG

The hill on the right is Kemmel. More distant, on the left, is the Messines-Wytschaete ridge, the battlefield of June 7th, 1917. The battle is in progress. Most to the left the ruins of Wytschaete village may be discerned through the ravaged trees of Wytschaete Wood. Between them and Kemmel may be made out the ruins of Messines. The drawing was made from the windmill on the little conical Scherpenberg knoll. The roof in the foreground is that of an old farmhouse which has never been abandoned by its tenant during nearly three years of exposure to German shell-fire. At daybreak on June 7th the farmer's family were all watching the battle from their windows. On Kemmel Hill, which is still more exposed, an old woman and her two young grandchildren have remained in their cottage throughout the war.

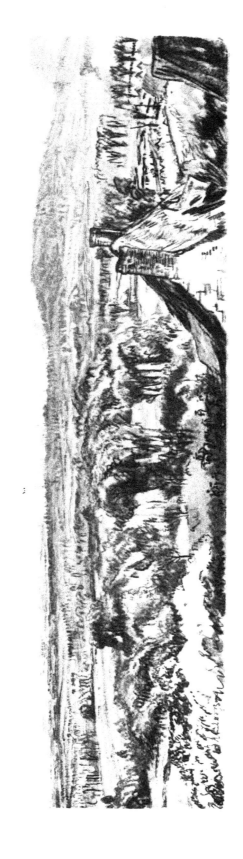

A STABLE ON THE WESTERN FRONT

A huge shed used temporarily as a stable. It made an uncommonly good one, as things go in war-time.

THE VIMY RIDGE, FROM NOTRE DAME DE LORETTE

The drawing shows clearly the general shape of the famous little ridge—the western slope on which the French gained a footing in June, 1915, and the crest over which the Canadians—British and French—drove the enemy eastwards at dawn on April 9th, 1917.

FIELD ARTILLERY SPORTS: THE RIVAL GUN TEAMS

A visitor who saw the faultless smartness and cleanness of the guns, the men, the horses and harness at these sports could hardly believe that they had only come out of action a few days before.

AN UNDERGROUND BILLET

Most billets anywhere near the front are underground.
This one is unusually serviceable. The ancient vaulted roof,
with any amount of protective ruins above it, can defy
the largest high-explosive shell; and the proportion of
external aperture to internal space is so small that a few
simple precautions can keep a great many men safe from
poison gas which, being heavier than air, tries to feel its
way down into cellars and dug-outs.

SCOTTISH PIPERS

A Highland battalion was taking its turn of rest behind the front at the time, and its pipers played every evening at Retreat, to the delight of the French villagers, who always turned out in their full available strength to listen to the music of their Celtic kinsmen.

A VIA DOLOROSA : MOUQUET FARM

The little white heap of ruins on the sky-line marks the site of the famous farm. The slope up which our men fought their way to it is marked with improvised memorials to a few of those who fell on the way. A similar series of these tragic and noble finger-posts points the way up from the valley of the Ancre to the heights of Thiepval. It is to be hoped that monuments so uniquely eloquent as these Stations of the Cross of soldierly self-sacrifice may not be suffered to disappear.

XLVIII

THE MEMORIAL ON THE FIELD
OF AGINCOURT

The artist found the village priest of Azincourt (as it is now spelt) acting as guide to a party of British officers, and showing them the positions of the British and French armies in the old battle. In approaching Agincourt, Henry V. and his army traversed the Somme battle-field of 1916, and the English king lodged for a night at Miraumont, on the Ancre, captured by the British from the Germans this spring, in a state of ruin. Bardolph's theft of the pyx in Shakespeare's " Henry V." was probably suggested by a contemporary record of a similar incident at or near Corbie, where the Ancre joins the Somme. The insistence of Shakespeare's Henry V., in the Agincourt campaign, on a policy of eschewing " frightfulness," even when he had the German pretext of " necessity " for it, has been a joy to many British soldiers engaged in the present war against calculated savagery.

XLIX

ON THE SEINE, BETWEEN ROUEN
AND HAVRE

One of the tit-bits of good fortune that—at any rate till recently—could befall a British soldier in France was to be shipped direct from Rouen to England with a wound not too severe to allow him to be on the deck of the hospital ship as she steamed slowly down the Seine. As the coils of the river unwind themselves before the cautiously advancing ship, there are placed before your eyes, during about seven hours, an almost bewildering series of beautiful spectacles in which the landscape, the architecture, the riverain life, and the character of the stream itself are so completely different from those of any other great river in Western Europe, that the most devout lover of the Thames or the Rhône can delight in them without feeling that his fidelity is being shaken.

BLOWN UP

The present state of the parish church of Athies, on the east of the Somme, south of Péronne. It is in the area evacuated by the Germans early in 1917, and was blown up by them before they retreated.

A RUINED CHURCH IN THE YPRES SALIENT : DISTANT YPRES

On June 7th, 1917, Ypres ceased to be in a salient, one horn of the crescent-shaped line of German positions round it being planed away by the capture of the Messines-Wytschaete ridge. These two drawings show the wide flat, with the ruined city in its midst, on which the Germans used to look down from their lines as the spectators look down on a stage from the dress circle of a theatre.

LII

AN OLD BILLET

The very Scottish-looking house, with a great dovecote in the upper part of its tower, has the date 1661 over the door. Like many other ancient houses of some pretension it is now a poor farm. The farmer is away on service in the French army, and all the work of the farm is done by his wife and children. British soldiers out of the line are billeted here from time to time.

A SUPPLY RE-FILLING POINT

A roadside " dump " to which the A.S.C. have brought supplies from the railhead. Here the food for man and beast remains under the charge of the A.S.C. until it is removed by the transport waggons of the several units of the division. The waggons on the right are loading with fodder for the divisional artillery horses.

LIV

DINNER TIME : MEN OF THE R.F.A.

The gunners of the New Army were surprisingly good during the battle of the Somme, but in the battles of this year their marksmanship has been far better. The infantrymen of an army will always be exacting critics of its gunners —it has sometimes been necessary to keep captured German gunners and infantry apart from each other in our lines—but after the battle of Messines our infantry had nothing but praise for the artillery barrages behind which they went into action.

LV

THE BACK GARDEN

It oftens happens that a trench passes through the ruins of a house, or is used to give safe access to some cellar or ruined building which is of service as a habitation, a machine-gun emplacement, or an observation post. Here an unobtrusive chimney is seen issuing from a cellar dug-out. The part of the house above ground was used by the French, and afterwards by us, as an observation post, but would not have offered safe quarters for troops.

LVI

AN ARMY RENDEZVOUS IN FRANCE

The creeper-covered yard of a quaint inn in a small, ancient French town. There is no luxury at this inn, and most of the waiting is done by one boy, but there is good wine, the cook has ardour and ingenuity, and thousands of officers fresh from the trenches have found the modest comfort of the place divine. When you have been long unused to them, a table-cloth, cutlery that shines, and a bed with sheets strike you as if they were new and delicious inventions.

LVII

SPITE

The garden of the house shown in the drawing of " The great Crater, Athies " (XXII). The surrounding country is well wooded and these woods offer excellent cover for troops against aerial observation. They were not felled by the Germans, but the ornamental trees in this garden were all carefully destroyed, though their value as cover for troops is trivial. The contrast forms a cutting comment on the German Staff's plea that the devastations which it ordered were reluctant sacrifices by humane men to military necessity or expediency.

LVIII

THE UNTILLED FIELDS

This, or something like it, meets the eye almost everywhere behind the Western front. The ghost of a dead village in the distance can be seen through, like the phantom ship in the "Ancient Mariner." The desolation, however, does not last. The old agriculture creeps steadily forward in the wake of the advancing Allied armies, and this summer good fields of grain are waving on land that looked almost hopelessly derelict last year. The work of reclamation has received much help from British military authorities who have instituted regular " agricultural departments " for the assistance of the returning farmers.

LIX

MEN OF THE R.F.A. CLEANING THEIR GUNS

When a battery comes out of the line to rest, its first form of repose is an orgy of gun-cleaning. The men of a good battery could no more settle down to any less strenuous recreation, while the guns were still dirty, than a Highland sergeant could take his ease in his inn while there was a patch not shining in the interior of his rifle barrel.

AN H.Q.

As a rule, the châteaux in the British zone cannot compare, for beauty, with those of middle and southern France, but here is one end of a beautiful house, lying among great woods far behind the line and used, when the drawing was made, as the head-quarters of some one or other of our many units.

SOLDIER'S TRAVEL

SIX of the drawings in this Part are of ships and they are their own introduction. A soldier who does not know the life of the sea can only say how they quicken the sense we all have of the hardness and fineness of naval service in this war, and of the capacity of great draughtsmanship to interpret them ; and also of the splendid and almost unknown services of those officers and men of the merchant marine to whose seamanship, power of command, and habits of discipline so many soldiers torpedoed or threatened on British transports owe their lives.

The rest of the drawings are diverse ; glimpses of the whole scene of war in Northern France, from the front to the sea. Every place drawn is one which a single British private might have seen on his way to the front, in his marching to and fro behind it, at his rest billets and, if he was hit, on his way to a home hospital. There is a fascination of its own about a soldier's travels in France. A fighting man, he is also a tourist who has to settle nothing for himself. When he lands perhaps he entrains in the dark, goes to sleep in the straw without knowing whether the train will go North, East, or South, an hour's run or a whole day's. It is like travelling on the Arabian Nights magical carpet, under sealed orders—only he does not go quite so fast. Perhaps he awakes in the first grey of the dawn and peers through a chink in the side of the truck and wonders where he is. Are they the Normandy apple orchards that he is passing, or the long chains of osier beds and water-cress lagoons under Picardy poplars, or are the devious roads those of Flanders, serpentining among the carefully drained fields ? If he knew the country in peace, he has great moments of recognition ; " Cities at cock-crow wake before him " ; he may espy, from five miles away, a dart of carved wood that he knows for the spire of Amiens Cathedral ; or it may be the blunt, buttressed tower of Bethune.

It is always merry travelling up to the front by day in a train. So long as the men adhere to the train when it moves, as they take care to do, their mode of adhesion is not so severely regulated as it is by the bye-laws of peace. Sometimes the foot board is thronged. There is an esteemed observation post at the end of each French truck, outside, a kind of crow's nest attained by a ladder. Gunners like to sit in the open, among the wheels of their lashed guns, with their legs dangling at ease over the low gunwale of the truck. During pauses the engine-driver is visited and some of his boiling water is diverted, by consent, from its ordinary propulsive task to the making of tea. Or, if there be snow on the ground, a company will fall to snowballing with the hands of a French factory, during their dinner hour, and part, when the train moves on, with wonderfully increased cordiality and respect for the marksmanship of both nations.

Then comes the detraining and with it perhaps the new soldier's first time of hearing the guns of the front. The fussy noise of the engine stops and the slow, rolling rumble from the eastern horizon can make itself heard. It sounds incredible at first with its almost sleepy dignity and its continuity ; it is to the ear what a long low range of dim blue hills is to the eye. And then the marching through towns and country always piquant to the foreign wayfarer, some of it written all over with legible history, modern and old. At Hesdin the buildings change ;

the westward-rolling wave of the old Spanish power printed some trace of its own likeness on them before it rolled back. You march on along the line of withdrawal until, in the Grande Place at Arras, you are, as it were, in full Spain. Or, as you march up the valleys of great French rivers, you see how the railways cling to the western bank, keeping the rivers between them and the eastern peril; and you think of the German northern railways set like a flight of arrows towards the Belgian frontier, so glaringly may the mere position of ballast and sleepers and steel write the history of half a century of insolent menace and of anxious self-protection.

The wounded or invalid soldier makes the reverse journey in a world of experiences remote from anything he has known. He may have had a few degrees of fever and awake from long nightmares of perplexed solitary wrestling in the dark with vast fancied responsibilities as a sentry, a runner, or a section commander, and find himself in a bed in a rich and curious oriental double tent, the gift of a king to our King, with a nurse accepting soothingly, in the sort of voice that he last heard in England, his assurances that he must get on at once about some sort of urgent trench business. Then there is mere rest, profound and unclouded and re-creating to body and mind, and then the kind of second boyhood that comes with every good recovery from serious illness, and then more travels; perhaps to Versailles when the leaves in the park are brown; perhaps to Rouen, where old France is most French and most interwoven with Norman England; perhaps to a hospital among pinewoods on the dunes; perhaps down the Seine to Havre, where the river pilot drops into a bobbing boat and goes off to his tug and ashore—and the next thing the British soldier may hear and see is the quiet lapping of the ripples of Southampton Water under the stationary ship's bows, and Netley among the trees on the starboard side. At any rate so it might be till the Germans treated hospital ships as fair game and the giant red cross and long tier of green lamps became a danger instead of a safeguard to nurses and wounded.

G. H. Q., France,
   August, 1917.

LXI

SPRING IN ROLLENCOURT VILLAGE

A typical French village in a valley behind the British front, at the time when the fruit trees begin to blossom. In passing through the hundreds of dust-covered ruins of villages where the Germans have been, it is almost impossible now to conceive that each of them once presented some such scene as this.

A SQUARE IN ARRAS

Many visitors to Arras during the war must have felt this square to be the most melancholy place in the desolate city. It was not ruined, but several houses were wounded by shells, and nearly all were empty; unheeded grass and weeds grew to extravagant heights among the stones, as in Piranesi's megalomaniac dreams of the Appian Way; the obelisk in the centre seemed oddly remote from human touch, like a peak in Darien ; and some acoustic property of the curved façades gave a peculiar resonance to the crash of occasional shells anywhere in the city or to the footfalls of some wayfarer coasting cautiously along close to the walls, to avoid enemy observation. Until the battle of Arras was fought, the nearest enemy trench was about 800 yards away.

LXIII

A VIEW OF ALBERT

From the West. The tree-lined road on the right is the great Route Nationale running from Rouen through Amiens, Albert, Pozières, Le Sars, and Bapaume to Mons and Valenciennes. The stretch of it seen in the drawing was under enemy observation until the battle of the Somme was fought. A screen used to be hung from tree to tree on the side nearest the spectator to hide the traffic to and from Albert. The leaning figure of the Virgin on the church tower of Albert is seen near the centre of the drawing.

A RAILHEAD

One of the points from which the army at the front is supplied with food and munitions. Some railheads are exposed to artillery fire, and casualties to officers and men occasionally occur as they do in the trenches, but the work is never interrupted for more than a few hours.

AN OFFICER'S BILLET

The house of which this is a part was built for one of
Napoleon's generals. It is a beautiful example of the
extreme refinement of the French architecture of its time.
A British officer or man on active service is lucky indeed
when such a billet falls to him.

LXVI

A HIGHLAND OFFICER

HESDIN

A corner of the cheerful main square of Hesdin. On the face of the buildings in the square may be read both the sixteenth century origin of the little town and the influence of the Spanish domination in the seventeenth century. The town hall, nearly filling one side of the square, is of a style akin to our own Jacobean ; and the quaint and rococo quality of many of the buildings has an entertaining effect like that of delightfully odd faces. The town has not been scarred by the war ; it is approached from all sides by roads sloping under fine trees ; it has many gardens full of roses and on its north is an ancient forest which still harbours wild boars.

TRANSPORT HORSES IN A FRENCH ORCHARD

The horses shown belonged to a Scottish division and had come out of the line somewhat thin and out of condition, but were recovering rapidly with rest and good grazing. The general condition of our transport horses is one of the successes of British military organisation in this war. It may also be boasted as some proof of national aptitude for horsemastership, a large proportion of the men in charge of the animals having had nothing to do with horses before the war.

AT AN A.S.C. DUMP

A corner of one of the depots to which stores are brought by the lorries and waggons of the Army Service Corps, thence to be distributed by the divisional transport to the various divisions at the front.

A RUIN AT VILLERS CARBONNEL

A point just behind the line from which the Germans were compelled to withdraw early in 1917. It lies south-west of Péronne and was taken over by the British from the French in the winter of 1916-17.

THE QUARRY NEAR MOUQUET FARM

This hollow was the only considerable place of shelter on the bald upland which has Mouquet Farm on its crest, between Thiepval and Pozières. The dug-outs seen in the drawing were made by the Germans and afterwards adapted and occupied by our troops. In the quarry are many British graves. The large one on the right is marked out with shells, and much trouble has been taken to set the cross with coloured stones. The fighting round Mouquet Farm was some of the hardest in the battle of the Somme.

LXXI

THE CHURCH AT FLERS

There was an extraordinary scene at Flers on September 15th, 1916, the first day when Tanks were used in war. A British Tank, driven with enthusiasm, made its way into Flers, ahead of the general advance, followed by a crowd of cheering and laughing infantry, and moved up and down the village street firing on the Germans still in occupation. Flers is now near the centre of a wide desert of thistles and poppies. The only living thing seen by the artist when making his sketch was the lurking cat gazing furtively at him from among the broken beams of a fallen roof. Inside the ruined church some broken images of saints have been carefully propped upright by passing soldiers.

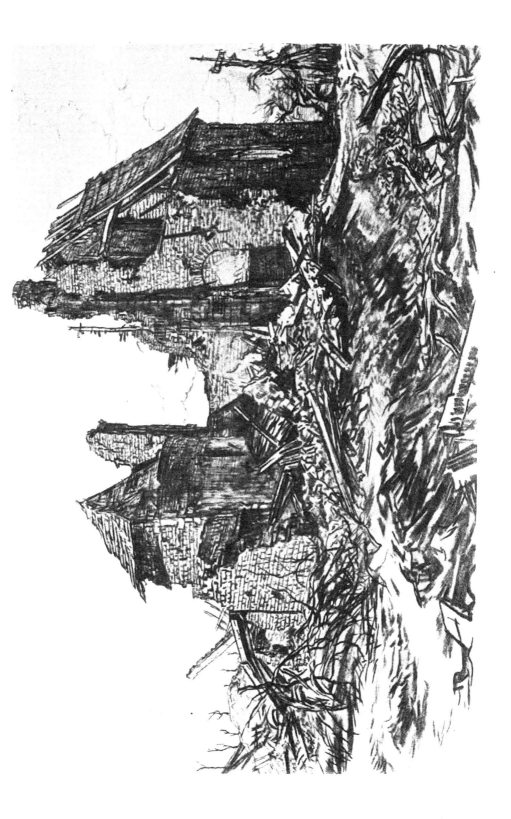

LXXII

IN THE SANTERRE

The fine, grave simplicity of this drawing is apt to the broad, bare austerity of the partly derelict plateau of Santerre, one of the most northern of the great grain lands of France. The trenches shown were made and first used by the French and afterwards held by British troops. The graves of two French soldiers are seen to the right, one of them marked with the dead man's steel helmet. In the distance are seen the remains of the woods about Estrées.

LXXIII

GOOD QUARTERS

The nucleus of the mass of ruins in the drawing is a bastion of the old château of Soyécourt, a village through which the front German and Allied lines ran at the opening of the Battle of the Somme. At the top of the pile may be noticed an artillery observation post. The security of the quarters for troops in the cellarage is guaranteed by the mass of débris above and by the presence of a second exit in case the first should be blocked by the explosion of an enemy shell.

LXXIV

OFF HAVRE: TAKING THE PILOT
ABOARD A HOSPITAL SHIP

Two sketches of the Seine scenery, passed by a Hospital Ship on its journey from Rouen to Havre, were reproduced as Plate XLIX. The present drawing shows the pilot being taken aboard at Havre for the voyage across the Channel. A rope ladder is thrown over the side of the ship to his little skiff below.

A DESTROYER AND LIGHT CRUISERS

Two types of ship which are sometimes confused by the landsman. He might plead in excuse the frequency with which new forms of each are evolved in the quest for higher speed and fighting power.

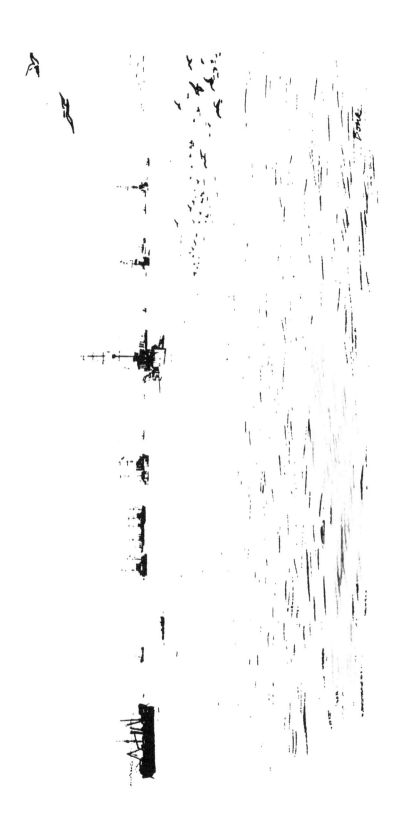

LXXVI

ON BOARD A BATTLE-CRUISER :
BETWEEN DECKS

The ship is the famous " Lion."   A bugler is seen in the
foreground.   Soldiers on active service in this war have,
as a rule, to do without the bugle calls which mark out
every portion of their day at home. Sailors are more
fortunate, and bugle calls on board ship gain a special
beauty from some acoustic property of the surrounding
water.

A DESTROYER IN A HARBOUR

Every British soldier on active service in this war is familiar with the lines of the destroyer, one of his chief visible safeguards on his journeys overseas.

FROM THE AFTER DECK OF A BATTLESHIP

The drawing expresses finely the way that man and even landscape seem to be dwarfed for the moment by one's sense of the massive puissance of a great battleship when one stands on its deck.

A LIGHT CRUISER : EVENING

Ours are said to be days of " floating fortresses," but sailors still cherish, as they have always done, the ideal of the Ship Beautiful, and many of them find it realized to-day in the light cruiser with her fine lines; yacht-like lightness and great speed. They never tire of praising her.

LXXX

THE BRIDGE OF A MERCHANT SHIP AT SEA

The nearest figure, examining a chart, is that of an officer who commanded a British transport, carrying troops, when it was torpedoed by a submarine at sea. His control of the situation, seconded by the thorough discipline of his crew and of the troops, secured the safety of almost everybody on board. The ship is not yet in open sea. The pilot is conning the vessel through the port defences. He stands close to the steersman, and both are intent on the work of keeping the fairway. Beyond the pilot, the officer of the watch is sweeping the distant sea horizon with his glasses, for the enemy has a way of hanging about a port's approaches. An apprentice stands behind the steersman, a sailor; on bridge look-out is posted on the extreme wing of the bridge. The keen faces intent on their work and look-out are typical of the Merchant Service, without whose effort and the pitting of their skill and seamanship against the enemy, the keen swords of Britain's warriors might be rusting in their island sheaths.

SHIP BUILDING

HERE are drawings, if not of the Western Front, yet of something without which there could be no Western Front, for Britain at any rate. Mr. Bone's art has always delighted most in inducing mazes of intricate details to yield effects of lucid, massive significance. His skill and his temperament are seen at their best in these wonderful aggregations of delicate minutiæ in which there is no confusion, no disproportion or indiscipline or straining for effect, but every touch of the pencil contributes in its measure to thrill you with the one feeling—" This, then, is how it is that many millions of men, from an island surrounded with venomous perils to ships, can carry on war overseas." There is the happiest correspondence between Mr. Bone's art, with its splendidly generalled armies of dutiful details, and an industry like ship building in which a puissant unity of result is produced by the orderly joint action of multitudes of ant-like workers, every one of them indispensable while every one is indescribably dwarfed by the hugeness of that which he helps to produce.

There are some kinds of manual work in which men do not easily take pride—work for which there is nothing to show, or only some trivial or rubbishy thing. It is not so with the building of ships. When the rivetter's heater-boy said, " Whaer wid the Loocitania hae been if it hadna been for me heatin' the rivets ? " he expressed a feeling that runs through the whole of a shipbuilding yard from the Manager down. It is a feeling that may have animated the journeyman mason who cut stones for the Campanile at Florence or the cathedral of Rheims. Each man or boy employed in building a liner or battleship feels himself to be a part-author of something organic, mighty, august, with a kind of personal life of its own and a career of high service, romance, and adventure before it. For him it comes to the birth on the day when it ceases to be an inert bulk of metal propped into position with hundreds of struts and dog-shores. At last the helpless rigid mass detaches itself quietly like an iceberg leaving the parent floe, and majestically assumes its prerogative of riding its proper element, serene, assured, and dominant. For the builder of ships nothing can stale the thrill of that moment or deaden his triumphant sense of parenthood. Long after the ship has gone out into the world from her narrow, smoky birthplace on the Tyne or Clyde he will follow her career in the newspapers, exult in her speed records, and hope and fear for her when disabled or overdue. The murder of the Lusitania drew thousands of men of all kinds from all parts of the country and Empire into the army. One hardly needs to be told that on Clydeside there were many set jaws and lowering brows when the news came in. Others had lost countrymen by the crime ; the men in that shipbuilding yard had also lost a child.

The modern changes in ship building have inevitably caused the work to gather itself into a few places. When hulls were of wood, and steam was not yet used, almost every seaport had its own building slips, and much of the building was done by men who would man and sail their handiwork when built, ships' carpenters making the hulls and sailormen masting and rigging them. When hulls came to be made of iron, and then of iron and steel, ship building had to go where coal and iron were, or whither they could be easily brought. With the size of hulls continually growing they had to be made, too, where a great ship could be launched. The Thames, with its strong tides, drastic scour, and splendid 30 ft. depth of channel at low water, has always had the second of these qualifications. To-day ship's plates are delivered in London at the same price as at Belfast and the use of electric power for driving machine tools has made the distance from coal a less serious drawback than before. Yet, for some reasons which are in dispute, ship building upon the great scale has passed away from the Thames to the Tyne and

Clyde, to Belfast and Barrow. The Clyde had the Lanarkshire iron and coalfields to draw on, Barrow the coal and iron of Northern and Midland England ; the Tyne had the coal on its banks and the iron within easy reach. As to depth of water, Barrow was on the sea ; the Tyne was so shaped that it scoured itself without dredging and could easily be canalised to give a depth of 30 feet, and the men of Glasgow and Belfast had learnt from the history of the Dee how a precious natural creek must be guarded from silting. When British ores began to run short a ship-building place had to be a large seaport, able to handle great foreign imports. For this the chief need was already supplied in each of these places, the depth and space of water required for launching ships being ample to float the incoming cargoes of ore. But now Glasgow and Belfast —the latter's ship building industry largely a kind of overflow meeting from Glasgow—were at a new advantage. As they had been further away than their rivals from enemy privateers in the Napoleonic wars, so now they were nearer to America. Many other circumstances, large and small, came in to turn a scale in favour of one or more of the elect seats of ship building. The Clyde has a specially fine and fast measured mile for speed trials. The Tynesiders came of a race of hard-bitten frontiers-men, people among whom an adventurous spirit, independence and readiness to run a wise risk or take a large responsibility were in the blood.

In most of these places the trade in ships has its own local features. At Barrow and on the Mersey the leaning has been to the building of warships and passenger vessels. On Tyneside the chief wares have always been cargo boats and the builders have given more thought to cargo-carrying power than to mere beauty of line, though every good shipbuilder, like every sailor, loves a handsome ship. On the Clyde they make everything—battleships, liners, tramps, ferry steamers, tugs, motor hospital launches, and what not. And they are proud of their versatile skill ; a working shipbuilder at Glasgow will laugh at some other place " where they build ships by the mile and cut them off as required."

(For anything that is of interest in this Introduction or in the notes to drawings in this Part, the writer is indebted to Captain D. W. Bone, to Mr. James Bone, or to the artist.)

G.H.Q., France,
   October, 1917.

LXXXI

LOWERING A BOILER INTO A SHIP

he interior of the shed shown in the drawing " On the
ocks " (XCI).   The ship's hull is complete and the time
r launching near.   To lower the huge weight of the
iler cannily into its home in the depths of the ship, a
mplicated and yet primitive system of tackle is employed.
here must have been some such arrangement of straining,
ljusting, and counter-straining lines and pulleys when
ontana raised the great obelisk in the Square of St.
ter's—only that then everyone present was ordered to
ep perfect silence so as " to cause no commotion in the
r," whereas in the building ship the clang of the hammers
incessant.

THE PLATERS' SHED

This is where the frames of the ship are cambered, or bent to the required curve, which is indicated by marks on the iron floor.

ON THE DECK OF A BIG SHIP

The ship drawn here is well advanced towards completion. The men employed on this deck are brought up to its level on a lift. The hose-like pipes running about the deck convey power for the pneumatic tools used by the rivetters.

BUILDING A LINER

The yard shown here had gradually expanded all round an ancient churchyard. The old church can be seen on the left, with the towering bows of the tall ship on the stocks beetling over it.

A SHAFT BRACKET

The brackets, on each side of the ship, hold the twin propeller shafts clear of the stern. The view here is from underneath.

SHIPYARD SEEN FROM BIG CRANE

The drawing was made from the top of the great " hammer-headed " crane shown in the drawing of " A Fitting-out Basin " (XC), the artist looking downward between the flanges of the jib. The size and solidity of the walls and bulkheads of the large ship on the stocks below make it seem almost more like a factory in the making than a ship.

LXXXVII

THE SEVEN CRANES

The wonders of modern shipbuilding, at its highest perfection, are to be seen in the fine scene here drawn. On the right a great ship is under construction. From all directions round it the cranes are swinging its plates to their destined places. The whole place presents a rousing spectacle of vast mechanical forces directed by human skill to the achievement of a multitude of difficult and delicate feats unified by one great purpose. It is like the Empire in this war.

LXXXVIII

PLACING AN OIL TANK IN A SHIP

Though less heavy than a ship's boiler, an oil tank is a ticklish thing to handle, and it takes some time, skill and watchfulness to hoist it safely into a ship and bed it neatly in its place.

IN THE ENGINE SHOP

The drawing shows a set of marine engines in process of erection in the workshop, before being installed in the ship.

A FITTING-OUT BASIN

In the fitting-out basin the machinery and heavy fittings are installed in a ship after her launching. To lift these great weights into the vessel there is used a " hammer-headed " crane much more powerful than the cranes used to carry material to its place on a vessel building on the stocks.

ON THE STOCKS

A large merchant vessel is being built under a shed, to shelter the hive of workmen beneath from the weather. The many little railways seen in the foreground bring the material from the " shops " to the stocks.

UNDERNEATH A SHIP

The hugeness of a modern liner's hull is never more imposing than when it is seen from underneath, while still on the stocks or in dry dock.

BUILDING A STANDARD SHIP

The interior of the hull is seen from the bows. The framing is not yet complete, and there are as yet no bulkheads dividing the ship into compartments.

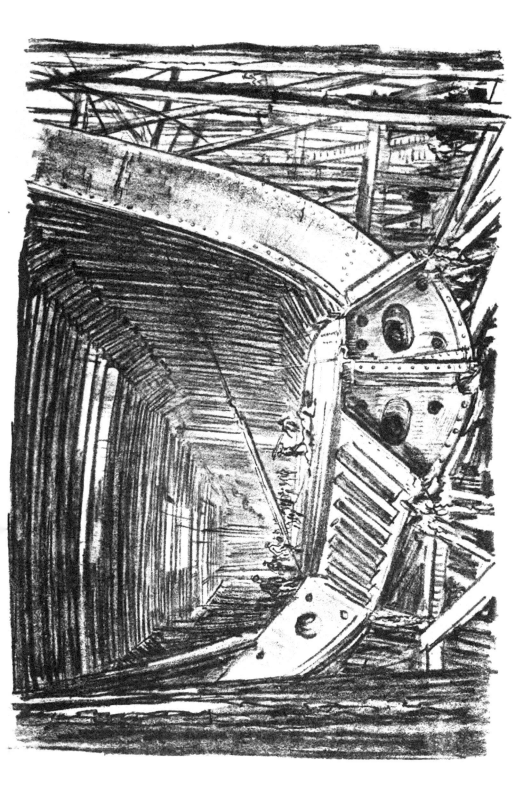

THE WORKSHOP

The large machines seen in the drawing are used for giving the required shapes to a ship's plates. This workshop, an old one, had been half rebuilt and its two parts presented a brilliant contrast of light and darkness, like that in Velazquez' " Tapestry Weavers."

A STANDARD SHIP IN A SHIPYARD BASIN

The standard ship is on the left. On the right are the bows of a large merchant vessel. The standard ships may not be beautiful in their lines, but their cargo-carrying capacity is admirable.

A SHIPYARD

On the right a large ship is being built. In these great yards there is constant change and improvement in the means for handling material, and two new cranes can be seen, partly built, in the centre of this drawing.

YARDS ON THE CLYDE

Two distinct yards are seen alongside each other. The quiet country scenery around them is a quite exceptional environment for a shipyard

RECONSTRUCTING A SHIPYARD

An old yard in process of modernisation. While work goes forward on a large ship, on the old stocks to the right, new slips are being built across the old dock on the left. Thus the work of shipbuilding never ceases while the whole yard is re-made.

READY FOR SEA

The ship shown has all but passed through the last stage of her infancy ; to-morrow she begins her active, independent life. There is great bustle about a ship at such a time ; her crew are busy taking stores aboard before the shipyard workmen have put the last touches to details of her equipment. It looks like chaos, but everything works up perfectly to the moment when she casts off, free of the seas.

A BIG LINER

A typical modern liner at a quayside. On the left are some old fishing craft.

THE
VESTERN FRONT

DRAWINGS BY
MUIRHEAD BONE

Bone

GERMAN PRISONERS
(Cover Illustration).

Watching the march past of German prisoners at the end of a day's battle on the Somme.

Another view of this scene is shown in Plate XXXIX.

WAR DRAWINGS

BY

MUIRHEAD BONE

DITION DE LUXE   Size 20 by 15 inches

r. Muirhead Bone's drawings in France are being reproduced under the title "The Western Front" (Monthly, 60 cents). In addition to this publication selection of drawings will be reproduced on a larger scale to give full effect the artist's work. There will be a series of parts, each containing ten ustrations, among which will be included some scenes in munition works in reat Britain. The drawings will be printed in one, two or more colours, cording to the character of the original.

TEN PLATES IN EACH PART

Contents of the First Part:

1. F.M. SIR DOUGLAS HAIG, G.C.B.
2. DISTANT VIEW OF YPRES
3. GRAND'PLACE & RUINS OF THE CLOTH HALL, YPRES
4. THE BATTLE OF THE SOMME
5. GORDON HIGHLANDERS, OFFICERS' MESS
6. A GUN HOSPITAL
7. "TANKS"
8. WATCHING OUR ARTILLERY FIRE ON TRÔNES WOOD FROM MONTAUBAN
9. AMIENS CATHEDRAL
0. THE NIGHT PICKET

Any of these subjects will be obtainable separately.

special large size facsimile reproduction, 28 by 20¼ inches, of Mr. Muirhead Bone's Superb Drawing of the "Tanks" will be obtainable.

Further particulars of these publications will
be sent on application to the Publishers—

GARDEN CITY, NEW YORK: DOUBLEDAY, PAGE & COMPANY.

CONTENTS.—Part II.

CONTENTS OF PART I.

INTRODUCTION BY

F.M. SIR DOUGLAS HAIG, G.C.B., G.C.V.O., K.C.I.E., **Я.**

GARDEN CITY, NEW YORK:
DOUBLEDAY, PAGE & COMPANY
1917.

The Western Front

CONTENTS OF THIS ISSUE

VOL. 2.   *PART II.*

DRAWINGS BY
MUIRHEAD BONE

GARDEN CITY, NEW YORK:
DOUBLEDAY, PAGE & COMPANY

The Western Front

CONTENTS OF THIS ISSUE

VOL. 2.   *PART III.*

GARDEN CITY, NEW YORK:
DOUBLEDAY, PAGE & COMPANY

1917.

The Western Front

CONTENTS OF THIS ISSUE

VOL. 2.   *PART IV.*

GARDEN CITY, NEW YORK:
DOUBLEDAY, PAGE & COMPANY
1917.

The Western Front

CONTENTS OF THIS ISSUE

VOL. 2.   *PART V.*

SD - #0129 - 020523 - C0 - 229/152/14 - PB - 9781333924577 - Gloss Lamination